JOHN QUINCY ADAMS

The Presidents of the United States

George Washington
1789–1797

John Adams
1797–1801

Thomas Jefferson
1801–1809

James Madison
1809–1817

James Monroe
1817–1825

John Quincy Adams
1825–1829

Andrew Jackson
1829–1837

Martin Van Buren
1837–1841

William Henry Harrison
1841

John Tyler
1841–1845

James Polk
1845–1849

Zachary Taylor
1849–1850

Millard Fillmore
1850–1853

Franklin Pierce
1853–1857

James Buchanan
1857–1861

Abraham Lincoln
1861–1865

Andrew Johnson
1865–1869

Ulysses S. Grant
1869–1877

Rutherford B. Hayes
1877–1881

James Garfield
1881

Chester Arthur
1881–1885

Grover Cleveland
1885–1889

Benjamin Harrison
1889–1893

Grover Cleveland
1893–1897

William McKinley
1897–1901

Theodore Roosevelt
1901–1909

William H. Taft
1909–1913

Woodrow Wilson
1913–1921

Warren Harding
1921–1923

Calvin Coolidge
1923–1929

Herbert Hoover
1929–1933

Franklin D. Roosevelt
1933–1945

Harry Truman
1945–1953

Dwight Eisenhower
1953–1961

John F. Kennedy
1961–1963

Lyndon B. Johnson
1963–1969

Richard Nixon
1969–1974

Gerald Ford
1974–1977

Jimmy Carter
1977–1981

Ronald Reagan
1981–1989

George H. W. Bush
1989–1993

William J. Clinton
1993–2001

George W. Bush
2001–2009

Barack Obama
2009–

JOHN QUINCY ADAMS

DAN ELISH

Other Marshall Cavendish Offices:
Marshall Cavendish International (Asia) Private Limited, 1 New Industrial Road, Singapore 536196 •
Marshall Cavendish International (Thailand) Co Ltd. 253 Asoke, 12th Flr, Sukhumvit 21 Road, Klongtoey
Nua, Wattana, Bangkok 10110, Thailand • Marshall Cavendish (Malaysia) Sdn Bhd, Times Subang, Lot
46, Subang Hi-Tech Industrial Park, Batu Tiga, 40000 Shah Alam, Selangor Darul Ehsan, Malaysia

Marshall Cavendish is a trademark of Times Publishing Limited

All websites were available and accurate when this book was sent to press.

Library of Congress Cataloging-in-Publication Data

Elish, Dan.
John Quincy Adams / Dan Elish.
p. cm. — (Presidents and their times)
Includes bibliographical references and index.
Summary: "Provides comprehensive information on President John Quincy Adams and
places him within his historical and cultural context. Also explored are the formative events
of his times and how he responded"—Provided by publisher.
ISBN 978-1-60870-182-7
1. Adams, John Quincy, 1767–1848—Juvenile literature.
2. Presidents—United States—Biography—Juvenile literature. I. Title.
E377.E45 2011
973.5'5092—dc22
2010013833

Editor: Christine Florie
Publisher: Michelle Bisson
Art Director: Anahid Hamparian
Series Designer: Alex Ferrari

Photo research by Thomas Khoo

The photographs in this book are used by permission and through the courtesy of: *Corbis:* 6, 10 r, 17, 23,
55; *Hip/Topfoto:* 59; *Library of Congress:* 89, 92; North Wind Picture Archives: 31; *The Bridgeman Art
Library: 3, 26*, 85, 95, 97 l; The Granger Collection/Topfoto: cover, 9, 10 l, 11, 13, 16, 19, 21, 27, 28, 33, 35,
36, 37, 38, 40, 41, 43, 47, 51, 52, 57, 60, 62, 64, 68, 73, 74, 76, 79, 81, 82, 87, 90, 91, 93, 96 (l & r), 97 r;
Ullstein bild/The Granger Collection, New York: 45

Printed in Malaysia
1 3 5 6 4 2

CONTENTS

John Quincy Adams was raised to live a life of public service. In 1824 he became the sixth president of the United States.

A Boy Born to Politics

Born into one of the leading families in the United States, America's sixth president, John Quincy Adams, bore the weight of great expectations. In April 1794 the future president received a letter from his famous father, John Adams, the **patriot** who became America's second president. The elder Adams wrote, "You come into life with advantages which will disgrace you if your success is mediocre. If you do not rise to the head not only of your profession, but of your country, it will be owing to your own *Laziness*, *Slovenliness*, and *Obstinacy*."

To his credit John Quincy Adams managed to exceed his father's lofty expectations. At the young age of fourteen he was chosen to be the chief aide to America's Russian ambassador. From that day until his death at age eighty, Adams served the United States as a foreign ambassador, senator, secretary of state, president, and finally congressman in the House of Representatives, where he distinguished himself by fighting against the expansion of slavery.

A man who commanded respect through his towering intellect, John Quincy Adams was admired more than liked. As he wrote about himself in his diary, "I am a man of reserved, cold, austere, and forbidding manners; my political adversaries say, a gloomy misanthropist, and my personal enemies, an unsocial savage."

But in the end what shines through about America's sixth president is his moral integrity. Time and again throughout his career Adams fought hard for what he believed, often in the face of opposition from his own party. Even so, he was extremely self-critical, once writing in his diary, "I am forty-five years old. Two-thirds of a long life have passed, and I have done nothing to distinguish it by usefulness to my country and to mankind."

Nothing could be further from the truth. Perhaps John F. Kennedy, America's thirty-fifth president, put it best when he noted in his book *Profiles in Courage* that "John Quincy Adams . . . held more important offices and participated in more important events than anyone in the history of our nation."

Boyhood in Braintree

John Quincy Adams was born on July 11, 1767, in Braintree (now Quincy), a town on the outskirts of Boston, Massachusetts. He was the second child of John and Abigail Adams. John Quincy's older sister was named after her mother but was known throughout her life as Nabby. In 1769 John Quincy had another sister, Susanna, who died at a little over one year of age. After that came two younger brothers—Charles, born in 1770, and Thomas Boylston Adams, born in 1772.

John Quincy's boyhood was marked by the long absences of his father, who traveled the surrounding area looking for legal work. By the early 1770s the elder Adams could often be found in Philadelphia, where he served as one of the leaders of the Continental Congress on the eve of the American Revolution. Still, John Adams took great interest in his children's upbringing, once writing to his wife, "Above all cares of this life let our ardent anxiety be to improve the minds and manners of our children. Let us

Quincy, Massachusetts (then part of Braintree), was the birthplace of presidents John Adams and his son John Quincy Adams.

teach them not only to do virtuously, but to excel." With her husband often away, Abigail Adams did her best, tutoring her first son from an early age.

As the eldest son, John Quincy liked to consider himself the man of the house, often asking to perform tasks usually reserved for older children. Before age ten he took it upon himself to ride by horseback between Braintree and Boston to retrieve the family mail, bringing praise from his father for seeing to "an office so useful to his Mamma and Pappa." Still, despite his obvious talents and ambition, Abigail fretted about her older son's impatience and tendency to be easily hurt—personality traits that he would carry into his adult life and career.

John Quincy's youth was marked by more than study and his attempts to make up for his father's long absences. By the time the boy was eight, tensions with England had grown to the point that war was a certainty. Terrified that British soldiers would raid Braintree, John Adams wrote to Abigail from Philadelphia that she should run for the woods with the children at the first sign of trouble. When the fighting came, it was on the other side of Boston, at Charlestown. Hearing cannon and musket fire, young John Quincy and his mother climbed up nearby Penn's Hill and saw smoke rising from the battlefield of Bunker Hill. Together,

John Quincy's parents, John Adams, second president of the United States, and Abigail Adams held high expectations of their children.

The Battle of Bunker Hill, fought on June 17, 1775, was one of the first major battles of the American Revolution. Though colonial forces were eventually forced to retreat, British troops suffered heavy casualties.

mother and son watched the first battle of the Revolutionary War in its entirety, an unforgettable event made more poignant when news arrived that a close family friend, Dr. Joseph Warren, the Adams's family physician, had been killed. Not long before, John Quincy had broken a finger so badly it was feared that it might have to be amputated. Dr. Warren had saved it.

A year later America declared its independence from Britain. As the battles spread throughout the colonies, young John Quincy focused on his studies. His sharp intelligence, coupled with feelings of inadequacy, shone through in a letter he wrote to his father at age nine:

Dear Sir:

I love to receive letters very well; much better than I love to write them. I make but a poor figure at composition. My head is much too fickle. My thoughts are running after bird's eggs, play and trifles, till I get vexed with myself. . . . I own I am ashamed of myself. I have but just entered the third column of Rollin's History. . . . I am determined this week to be more diligent.

I wish, sir, you would give me in writing some instructions with regard to the use of my time, and advise me how to proportion my studies and play, and I will keep them by me, and endeavor to follow them.

With the present determination of growing better, I am, dear sir, your son,

John Quincy Adams

THE AMERICAN REVOLUTION

When early colonists from England settled in the New World, they were perfectly content to live under the rule of the British crown. That began to change with the French and Indian War (1754–1763), in which British troops won control of Canada. When the battles were over, King George III and the English Parliament found the wars had cost a great deal of money. Deeply in debt, the king and Parliament decided that the

American colonists should help foot the bill. In 1765 Parliament passed the Stamp Act, a law that forced colonists to pay a tax on paper goods ranging from newspapers to playing cards.

Many colonists—who now thought of themselves as Americans—weren't pleased. Not allowed seats in Parliament, they decried what they called "taxation without representation." As tensions mounted and taxes increased, many Americans began to think that the colonies would be better off as an independent nation.

Due to the power of his intellect and forceful manner, John Adams soon became one of the leaders of the American Revolution. In 1776 Thomas Jefferson penned the Declaration of Independence. Signed on July 4 by the other delegates to the Continental Congress (below), the famous document asserted America's independence from Great Britain.

Soon enough, John Quincy would have ample opportunity to prove himself to his father. In December 1777, with the war with Britain raging, the Continental Congress assigned John Adams to Paris to join Benjamin Franklin. Together they would promote the American cause for independence. At first Abigail wanted the entire family to make the trip. But her husband was worried about the danger. What if the family was caught by an English ship on the high seas? Determined to accompany his father, John Quincy begged to go until his father agreed. On February 13, 1778, father and son set sail for Paris aboard the twenty-four-gun Continental frigate *Boston*.

ON TO EUROPE

Today, a jet can fly from Boston to Paris in seven hours or less. At the time of the revolution, crossing the Atlantic Ocean was much more difficult. At first John Quincy occupied himself by studying French with a Parisian doctor who was also onboard. But in late February a storm smashed the boat for three days straight, making both Adamses seasick. John Quincy's father wrote in his journal, "To describe the ocean, the waves, the winds, the ship, her motions, rollings, wringings, and agonies—the sailors, their countenances, language, and behavior is impossible." Lightning killed a man on deck. John Adams wrote, "No place or person was dry." Later, the *Boston* was attacked by a pirate ship. Throughout the journey the elder Adams was proud of his son's behavior, writing, "[F]ully sensible of our danger [in the storm], [John Quincy] was constantly endeavoring to bear under it with a manly courage and patience."

On April 1, 1778, the *Boston* docked in Bordeaux, France. Traveling overland, they arrived in Paris on April 8 and soon accepted Benjamin Franklin's invitation to stay in his home. As the elder Adams worked, John Quincy attended a local school, which he seemed to enjoy despite the fact that classes started at 6 AM. Most impressive was his continued mastery of French. John Adams wrote that his son "learned more French in a day than I could learn in a week with all my books." John Quincy also developed a lifelong love of theater, especially comedy.

Time passed quickly. After a year John Adams's **diplomatic** mission came to an end, and on August 2, 1779, father and son returned to Braintree. Home only briefly, Congress ordered John Adams back to Paris again, this time to seek treaties with England. John Quincy, now twelve, wanted to attend an

LETTERS FROM HOME

Though John Quincy spent a good chunk of his boyhood overseas, his mother, Abigail, made sure to keep a close eye on his behavior. Worried that her son might turn out like her brother, who had abandoned his wife and children and died an alcoholic, she wrote to John Quincy that he must never disgrace her and always be well behaved.

At her most strident she wrote, "For dear as you are to me, I had much rather you should have found your grave in the ocean you have crossed, or any untimely death crop you in your infant years, rather than see you an immoral profligate or a graceless child."

For his part John Adams did his best to reassure his wife that their child was well behaved, writing home, "My son gives me great pleasure . . . the lessons of his Mamma are a constant law to him."

American school in preparation for attending Harvard. But this time his mother insisted that he return to Europe, arguing that the opportunity to learn about foreign affairs and diplomacy was too good to pass up. And so John Quincy returned to Europe, this time with his younger brother Charles.

Soon after arriving back in Paris, John Adams became convinced that members of the French foreign ministry were blocking his efforts at making peace with Britain. As a result, he decided to try his luck in persuading the Dutch government to recognize American independence. On July 27, 1780, father and son set off for Holland. (By that point young Charles had returned home to Boston.) Soon John Quincy found himself enrolled at the University of Leiden in Holland. Though his father's work often took him to other countries, he kept in close touch with his son about his studies, once urging him to read more English poets. Perhaps most important, John Quincy learned to speak Dutch to go along with his French.

An esteemed member of America's Continental Congress, Francis Dana was head of a committee that visited Valley Forge in the winter of 1778 to help George Washington reorganize the colonial army. In 1781, John Quincy Adams served as Dana's aide in Russia.

Soon enough, the boy was deemed ready for his first diplomatic assignment. Over the summer of 1781 Francis Dana, a friend of the Adams family, was ordered by Congress to travel to the court of Catherine the Great of Russia to

Ruling Russia from 1762 until her death in 1796, Catherine the Great oversaw the modernization of her country. Under her rule, Russia took its rightful place on the world stage.

convince her to recognize America as an independent nation. Dana needed an aide who could speak French, the language of international diplomacy, and John Adams suggested his son. On July 7, 1781, Dana and John Quincy Adams boarded a carriage and began a 2,000-mile trek to Saint Petersburg, Russia.

The Teenage Diplomat

Today, the United States is one of the most powerful nations in the world. But it took time for the young country to gain the world's respect. As a result, Francis Dana and John Quincy Adams's long journey to Saint Petersburg was largely for naught. Despite their repeated attempts, Catherine the Great refused to see them. In fact, the two Americans spent a full year in the city without making official contact with any member of the Russian government. John Quincy, ever industrious, used the time as best he could, reading book after book and learning to speak German to go along with his fluent French and Dutch.

On October 30, 1782, John Quincy finally left Russia, traveling through Sweden, Denmark, and northern Germany, making his way to the Hague, the capital city of Holland, where his father had been sent to arrange a loan from the Dutch to the U.S. government. In the two years he had been away, John Quincy had grown into a handsome young man of medium height, with a strong jaw and a stocky, if a bit pudgy, frame. Like his father's, his hairline began to recede when he was young.

Over the next two years John Quincy continued his studies in Holland and France. In mid–May 1784 his mother and sister, Nabby, traveled to Europe to visit. John Adams wrote his wife that their son was "the greatest traveler of his

At age sixteen, John Quincy Adams was already fluent in French, Dutch, and German.

age, and without partiality, I think as promising and manly a youth as is in the world."

With mother and sister safely in Europe, the Adams family settled in France, where the elder John had been called to join Thomas Jefferson and Benjamin Franklin in negotiating trade treaties with various European nations. Settling in the Parisian countryside, talk quickly turned to young John's future. It was soon decided that after seven years in Europe, it was time for John Quincy to return to the states. Arrangements were made for the young man to study at Harvard. In May 1785 he boarded a ship for America and sailed for home.

*W*hen John Quincy Adams arrived back in Boston to begin classes, he received a rude blow. Though the young Adams was fluent in French, Dutch, and German, Harvard president Reverend Joseph Willard insisted that he spend the winter reviewing his Latin and Greek, then come back for more testing in the spring. Six months of difficult study with an uncle in nearby Haverhill followed. That March Adams returned to Cambridge.

A Westerly View of The Colledges in Cambridge New England
A *Harvard Hall*   B *Stoughton*   C *Massachusett*   D *Hollis*   E *Holden Chapel*

John Quincy was one of five U.S. presidents who received his undergraduate education at Harvard University. The others were his father, Theodore Roosevelt, Franklin Roosevelt, and John Kennedy.

After a brief but difficult examination, Reverend Willard announced, "You are admitted, Adams." Finally, John Quincy Adams was a Harvard man.

Though Adams became one of the leading politicians and diplomats of his day, in college he enjoyed math and the sciences as well, taking classes in algebra and astronomy. But he also found time for simpler pleasures, occasionally skipping classes to fish or play the flute. In the end, however, Adams put his nose to the grindstone and ultimately was elected to the academic honor society Phi Beta Kappa. Meeting with fellow scholars, he gave talks on topics of the day, ranging from the origin of ideas to "Whether love or fortune ought to be the chief inducement to marriage." Taking a position that was forward-looking for the era, he argued that single women ought to be allowed to make romantic overtures to men they were attracted to.

Adams graduated on July 18, 1787. The second in his class, he gave a stirring address at the ceremony titled "Upon the importance and necessity of public faith to the well-being of a community." Afterwards, his family rented out two of the largest rooms in Cambridge to accommodate more than one hundred guests, including the governor, who came to celebrate. President Willard wrote Adams's parents, "[John's] attention to his studies, proficiency in literature, strict conformity to the rules of the University, and purity of morals have gained him the high esteem of the governors of this society and indeed of all his acquaintances. . . . I think he bids fair to become a distinguished character."

Indeed, Adams's college years were relatively happy. But his next expected step in life was law school, something he looked to with little enthusiasm.

The Constitutional Convention

After the American Revolution the United States was run by the Articles of Confederation, a series of laws that gave power to the states at the expense of the central government. By the time John Quincy Adams was graduating college, it was generally agreed that the country required a new constitution that featured a stronger central government able to make laws, collect taxes, and support an army. In 1787 delegates from across the country met in Philadelphia (below). Led by James Madison, who became the country's fourth president, America's current constitution was formulated and passed into law. The Constitution created the executive branch, or the presidency; the judicial branch, or the Supreme Court; and the legislative branch, or the two branches of Congress—the Senate and the House of Representatives. In 1789 George Washington was elected the first president of the United States.

Hard Times

The next seven years were not happy ones for Adams. In those days a young man interested in studying law didn't go to school but **apprenticed** with a working lawyer. Though the elder John Adams considered returning from England, where he was still stationed as a diplomat, to teach his son, it was decided that John Quincy Adams could be suitably trained by Theophilus Parsons, an attorney who lived in Newburyport, 40 miles northeast of Boston. Accordingly, on September 7, young Adams boarded a stagecoach for his new home. Quickly he found that legal study did not agree with him. Parsons assigned his apprentices twelve hours of reading a day. The workroom was cramped, noisy, and poorly heated.

Despite the less than ideal working conditions, Adams continued to put inordinate pressure on himself. His diary of the period is filled with passages in which he scolds himself for falling short of the goals set by his parents and himself. By the autumn of 1788 he wrote, "I felt a depression of the spirits to which I have hitherto been entirely a stranger." Unable to work, Adams returned to Braintree that October to recover, finally feeling well enough to return to school the following March.

Back in Newburyport Adams's spirits soon lifted—but not due to any renewed passion for his legal studies. Rather, for the first time in his life, Adams fell in love. Mary Frazier was the daughter of a prominent local couple. Though not yet sixteen, she was considered one of the great beauties of the town, and it wasn't long before a joyous side to Adams's personality not often remembered shone forth. Adams was so smitten that he wrote his beloved a poem. Titled "A Vision," its last verse went like this:

On thee thy ardent lover's fate depends,
From thee the evil or the boon descends;
Thy choice alone can make my anxious breast
Supremely wretched, or supremely blest.

But Adams's first great love was to end in deep disappointment. When his mother found out that her eldest son had met someone, she wasn't pleased. "Common fame reports that you are attached to a young lady," she wrote him. "I am sorry that such a report should prevail." She went on, "Never form connections until you see a prospect of supporting a family . . . a too early marriage will involve you in troubles that may render you and yours unhappiness the remainder of your life."

Still financially dependent on his parents, Adams felt he had no choice but to end the relationship. It was a cruel blow. In fact, after the breakup Adams never mentioned Mary again until a diary entry written when he was seventy years old, after accidentally stumbling upon her grave. He wrote that after they parted, "four years of exquisite wretchedness followed . . . nor was the wound in my bosom healed till the Atlantic Ocean flowed between us."

PUBLICOLA

In the summer of 1790 John Quincy Adams opened a law office in Boston. It wasn't long, however, before events conspired to push him into his natural calling: politics. In 1789 much of the talk on the streets of America was of the French Revolution. That year the French monarchy had been overthrown and replaced by a government of the people, based on a constitution.

Thomas Paine

In the fall of 1774 a boat from Europe docked in Philadelphia's harbor. Onboard was an Englishman named Thomas Paine who had made the trip to America hoping to change his fortunes. At age thirty-seven Paine was an out-and-out failure. But stepping onto American shores, all of that would change. In 1776 Paine published a pamphlet called *Common Sense*, an essay that laid out in clear language why America should be independent from Britain. Read by hundreds of thousands of Americans, *Common Sense* became the country's first best seller. Within one year, more than twenty-five editions were printed. Later, at the dawn of the French Revolution, Paine wrote *The Rights of Man*, a document that prompted John Quincy Adams to respond with his own series of political essays attributed to Publicola.

Unfortunately, the revolution also came with a brutal reign of terror during which thousands of opponents of the state were guillotined. Many Americans were appalled by the violence. Others supported the French Revolution in spirit, even if they didn't approve of the methods of the revolutionaries. One of the most ardent supporters of France was Thomas Jefferson, who criticized those who had broken with the true faith of the American "revolutionary path."

Execution of royalists was common during the French Revolution.

Adams was outraged. Assuming that Jefferson was criticizing his father's more conservative pro-British viewpoint, Adams fired off a series of eleven essays that argued that the U.S. Constitution was superior to the doctrines of the French Revolution. Where Thomas Paine's essay *The Rights of Man* argued that laws should reflect "the will of the majority," Adams insisted that a constitution had to protect the rights of the minority.

Adams penned another series of essays that appeared under the name Marcellus in April and May of 1793. A subsequent group of essays was attributed to Columbus and came out in November and December. Another group, attributed to Barneveld, appeared in the *Boston Chronicle* in December 1793 and January 1794.

This portrait of John Quincy Adams was completed around the time he was ambassador to Holland.

At first some readers assumed the Publicola essays were written by John Quincy Adams's father. But soon enough the son got the credit he deserved. One person who was especially impressed was President George Washington. The first president clearly felt that Adams's experience and intellect could be put to good use by the U.S. government. In 1794 Washington appointed Adams as the ambassador to Holland. Adams's father was thrilled.

THE YOUNG DIPLOMAT

As was his nature, John Quincy Adams greeted his appointment less with excitement than with worry. "I wish I could have been consulted before it [the appointment] was irrevocably made," he said. "I rather wish it had not been made at all."

In the end Adams accepted the position, but not before convincing his younger brother, Thomas Boylston, to accompany him as his secretary. In September the two brothers set off aboard a leaky boat called the *Alfred* and made a swift trip to England, luckily missing a giant storm that destroyed a host of sturdier ships.

John Quincy Adams reported for duty in the Netherlands on October 31, 1794. Once again England and France were at war. The invading French army had thrown the Netherlands into turmoil. As ambassador, Adams sent reports on the situation back to Washington while doing his best to protect the rights of American citizens abroad.

That fall Adams was ordered to travel to London on official business. After seeing to his duties, he stopped at the home of Joshua Johnson, the American consul to London and the father of seven daughters. There Adams met the second eldest,

Near Disaster in England

Adams's first assignment as a diplomat was to deliver a trunk full of State Department dispatches to John Jay, the U.S. ambassador in London. Making their way over London Bridge in the half darkness, the brothers heard a loud thump. John Quincy looked back over his shoulder to see a dreadful sight: the trunk of documents was missing.

Terrified, the brothers had the carriage stop and looked frantically for the valuable dispatches. Luckily, the trunk was directly underneath the carriage, where it had fallen. John Quincy shook with relief. To fail at his very first assignment would have been terribly embarrassing. After all, the dispatches had been handed to him by George Washington himself.

Louisa. By Christmas Adams was a regular visitor at the Johnson home. By February the next year he worked up the courage to profess his feelings. Though Louisa's response was positive, in truth she was as surprised as she was pleased. Adams was so quiet about his intentions, Louisa assumed that he was interested in her older sister.

As with her son's first love, Abigail Adams did not approve, writing to her son that he should wait to marry in the United States. This time Adams ignored her, writing to his mother that Louisa had "goodness of heart and gentleness of disposition, as well as spirit and discretion." Though Adams's duties in Holland kept them apart for a time, the couple was finally wed on July 26, 1797.

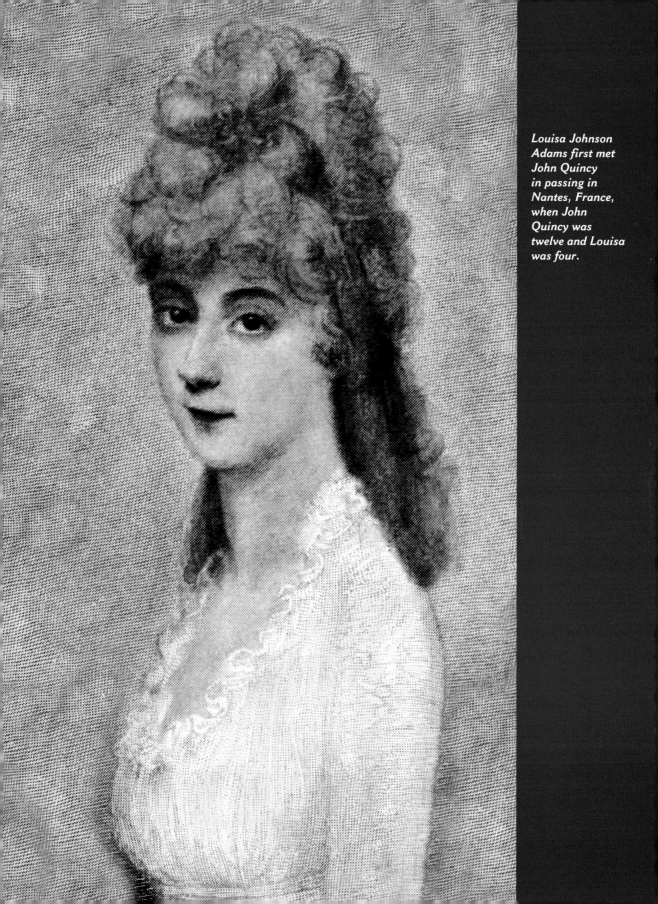

Louisa Johnson Adams first met John Quincy in passing in Nantes, France, when John Quincy was twelve and Louisa was four.

A month before his marriage Adams had been asked to be minister to Portugal. But soon thereafter George Washington's two terms as president drew to a close, and Adams's father was elected to be the second president of the United States. Upon taking office, the elder Adams considered withdrawing John Quincy from the foreign service, thinking it would look unseemly to keep his own son in an important job. But none other than George Washington disagreed and urged him to keep John Quincy in the position. In the end John Adams reassigned John Quincy Adams to be America's ambassador to Prussia.

While spending four years with Louisa in Berlin, Adams successfully negotiated trade agreements between the two countries. But in 1800 his father was defeated for a second term as president by Thomas Jefferson. The following year Adams, his wife, and infant son, George, sailed back to the United States to start a new life.

TROUBLE GETTING INTO TOWN

The trip John Quincy and Louisa Adams took to Prussia turned into a test of endurance. Though the first leg of the journey from London to Hamburg by sea went smoothly enough, the couple was forced to travel the rest of the way by stagecoach over muddy roads, staying in inns with bedbugs. But that wasn't the worst. When the Adamses finally arrived at the gates of Berlin, the lieutenant on duty refused them entrance, claiming that the United States didn't exist. Finally, another soldier who had heard of America let the Adamses through the gates and into the city.

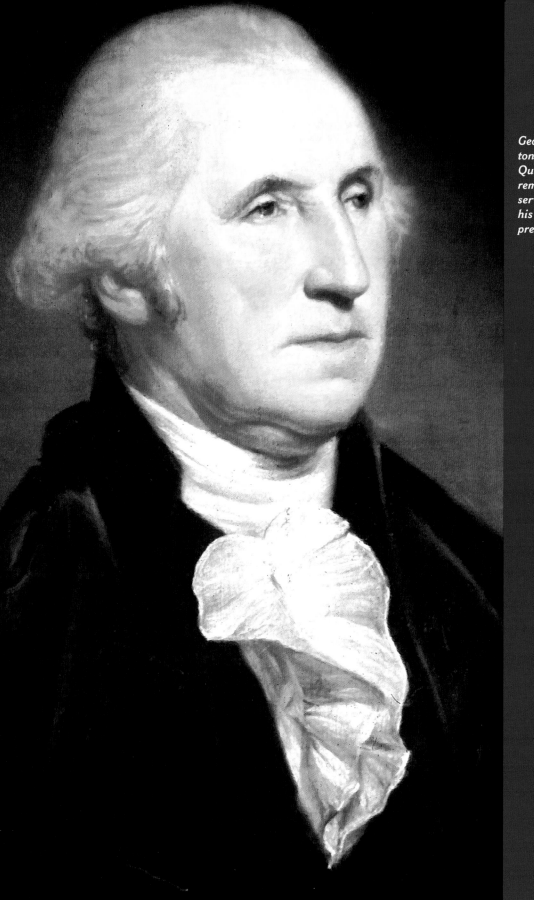

George Washington believed John Quincy should remain in foreign service during his father's presidency.

Adams Takes a Stand

*J*ohn Quincy Adams returned to a divided country. During his presidency George Washington had become aligned with his powerful secretary of the Treasury, Alexander Hamilton. Together they headed the **Federalist Party**, composed of Americans who believed in a strong central banking system and government. At the same time Thomas Jefferson and James Madison aligned to become the leaders of the **Jeffersonian-Republicans**, Americans who believed that the bulk of the power in the country belonged with the individual states. In general, southerners, westerners, and farmers were Jeffersonian-Republicans. Residents of the states of New England and city dwellers tended to support the Federalists.

While the members of the two parties held different views on a range of **domestic** issues, from how to pay off war debt to the location of the nation's capitol, they also differed in their view of foreign affairs. In 1793 Britain and France went to war. Most Jeffersonian-Republicans remained loyal to the French, who had come to the colonists' aid during the American Revolution, while the Federalists favored England. As hostilities between the nations intensified, both England and France began to stop and board American merchant ships. Worse, the British "impressed" American sailors, forcing them to join the British navy. Americans were understandably furious. But George Washington did

Britain helped provoke the War of 1812 by impressing American sailors.

whatever he could to keep the United States neutral, often upsetting the Jeffersonians, who wanted the United States to join the war on the side of the French.

In 1800 Thomas Jefferson ran to unseat John Adams as president. The once-close friends who guided the former colonies to their independence turned into bitter rivals. When Jefferson won a narrow victory, his supporters applauded what they called the end of the "Federalist Reign of Terror." Some sang a song titled "Jefferson and Liberty":

> *Lord! How the Federalists will stare*
> *At Jefferson, in Adams's chair!*

Like his father, John Quincy Adams was a Federalist, believing firmly in a strong central government whose law trumped that

The presidential campaign of 1800 was one of the most bitter in American history. Supporters of Thomas Jefferson created this anti-Adams banner.

of the individual sates. But for the rest of his career, Adams would prove himself to be that rare politician: a **maverick** who didn't always follow the party line but formulated his views on the merits of each individual issue as it arose. He was even willing to side with Thomas Jefferson, the man who had ousted his father from the White House.

Soon after his arrival back in the United States, the younger Adams would find his strong moral convictions put to the test. In February 1803 the Federalist-controlled Massachusetts legislature elected him to a six-year term in the U.S. Senate.

THE SENATE YEARS

Within days of taking his seat on the Senate floor, Adams demonstrated his independent streak. In 1803 France controlled the Louisiana Territory, an enormous tract of land to America's west. Worried that French ruler Napoléon Bonaparte might use the territory as a base from which to

John Quincy Adams as he looked as a young senator.

invade the United States, President Jefferson sent James Madison, his secretary of state, to France to see if America could buy the city of New Orleans to ensure American shipping rights along the Mississippi River. Focused on the war with Britain, Napoléon offered the United States the entire Louisiana Territory for the relatively small sum of $15 million, a real estate deal that increased America's size by 828,000 square miles.

Jefferson and his party jumped at the chance to expand America's borders. But the Federalists of New England were strongly opposed to it, worried that a larger nation would dilute

Sometimes called the greatest real estate deal in world history, the Louisiana Purchase increased the size of America by 828,800 square miles.

their economic and political power and possibly provide Jefferson with a permanent **majority** in Congress. Despite his Federalist leanings, Adams was quick to support the purchase, arguing that the United States needed to expand in order to become a great power. Federalists fumed. "Curse on the stripling [the son]," one cried. "How he apes his sire [father]!"

Adams held firmly to his beliefs but still appreciated it when his father wrote to him, affirming his support: "I do not disapprove of your conduct in the business of Louisiana, though I know it will become a very unpopular subject in the northern states . . . I think you have been right!"

A few months later Adams wrote in his diary about the downside of America's two-party system—complaints that still ring true today.

I have already had occasion to experience, which I had before the fullest reason to expect, the danger of adhering to my own principles. The country is so totally given up to the spirit of party that not to follow blindfolded the one or the other is an expiable offence.

As fit his character, Adams continued to support the policies that he thought were best for the country as opposed to his party. And it wasn't long before he managed to infuriate fellow Federalists once again.

During the first decade of the 1800s U.S. foreign policy was marked by Britain's continued disrespect of American shipping rights. Time and again American merchant ships were stopped on the high seas. British captains continued to impress American sailors into the British navy. While many Federalists, who still supported England, chose to look the other way, Adams was enraged.

EARLY WASHINGTON, D.C.

The Washington, D.C., of the early 1800s wasn't nearly as magnificent as it is today. When Thomas Jefferson was elected president, there was only one recognizable street, today's New Jersey Avenue. Pennsylvania Avenue, on which the White House now sits, did not yet exist. The space between the president's home and Congress was covered with alder bushes. Cows grazed in the streets, and hogs snorted through the mud. Corn grew by homes. The city was routinely called "a capital of miserable huts."

In 1806 he pushed through Congress a series of **resolutions** condemning British actions. He also supported a bill that limited British imports into American harbors.

But the stakes soon became higher. In 1807 a U.S. frigate, the *Chesapeake*, was stopped by a British warship named the *Leopard*, whose captain demanded that the American captain turn over four sailors thought to be British deserters. The captain of the *Chesapeake* refused, and the British ship opened fire. In the end three men were dead, eighteen were wounded, and the British took the four sailors.

Britain impresses more American sailors following the defeat of the USS Chesapeake *by the HMS* Leopard *on June 22, 1807.*

In retaliation, on December 22, 1807, the Jefferson administration passed the **Embargo** Act, a law that called for an immediate halt to all American shipping to Europe in order to force Britain to respect American rights on the seas. Though the bill was the brainchild of John Adams's political rivals, Thomas Jefferson and James Madison, it was John Quincy Adams who rose instantly to the Senate floor to shout his support. Later Adams said to a colleague, "This measure will cost you and me our seats."

Adams was right. As it turned out, the Embargo Act was a failure. Not only did the British keep impressing American sailors, the law devastated New England manufacturing. Unable to trade legally with England and France, smugglers ran goods to Canada and then Europe. In 1808 American **exports** stood at barely one-fifth of what they were a year earlier. Needless to say, Adams was deeply unpopular in his home state. The Northampton *Hampshire Gazette* called him "A party scavenger! . . . one of those ambitious politicians who lives on both land and water, and occasionally resorts to each, but who finally settles down in the mud." One Bostonian even refused to attend the same party, saying, "I would not sit at the same table with that renegade."

Though reviled by Federalists far and wide, Adams took some solace from the words of his father, who wrote, "[Y]ou have too honest a heart, too independent a mind, and too brilliant talents, to be sincerely and confidentially trusted by any man who is under the domination of party maxims or party feelings."

Adams stuck to his guns, insisting until the bitter end that England's warlike behavior must be stopped. Unforgiving, the Massachusetts legislature voted in a new senator nine months

A political cartoon shows Thomas Jefferson's pockets being picked by King George of England and Napoleon of France as a result of his ill-fated embargo policy.

before Adams's term was up, in effect leaving him no choice but to resign. Still, he wrote that "far from regretting any one of those acts for which I have suffered, I would do them over again . . . at the hazard of ten times as much slander, unpopularity, and displacement."

Back to Russia

The year after being forced out of the Senate, Adams wrote and lectured at Harvard. But soon enough another political appointment arrived. On March 4, 1809, James Madison became America's fourth president and promptly named Adams the nation's ambassador to Russia.

By this time Adams and Louisa were the parents of three sons, George Washington Adams, eight; John Adams II, six; and the youngest, Charles. With the two older boys boarding with relatives in Massachusetts, John Quincy, Louisa, little Charles, three secretaries, and two servants boarded the merchant ship *Horace* on August 5, 1809, and departed for Saint Petersburg. On the way Adams wrote a long letter to the two sons who remained behind in the United States, urging them to strive for greatness in much the same way his father had urged him. "Make your talents and your knowledge most beneficial to your country," he wrote, "and most useful to mankind."

Adams and crew reached Saint Petersburg exactly eighty days after departing. Adams was impressed with the changes in the city since his last visit in 1782. One of Europe's grandest cities, Saint Petersburg then boasted a population of 400,000 people. The most welcome change was Russia's attitude toward the United States. Whereas thirty years earlier the fourteen-year-old Adams and his superior Francis Dana hadn't been allowed a single meeting with a member of the Russian government, now Adams became fast friends with Alexander I, a czar known for his open mind and humane policies. Soon the two men could be seen walking the streets of Saint Petersburg, chatting.

Czar Alexander I and John Quincy became fast friends while Adams was stationed in Russia.

Justice Adams?

John Quincy Adams served the U.S. government in virtually every important position. But it is little remembered that he also could have been a Supreme Court justice. In 1810, while Adams was serving in Russia, President James Madison offered to nominate him to the high court. After due consideration Adams, who never really liked the law, turned down the offer. As he wrote to his brother, "I am also, and always shall be, too much of a political **partisan** for a judge."

Alexander I even gave Adams permission to appear in the royal court without his wig.

As it turned out, Adams was stationed in Russia during turbulent times. In April 1812 Napoléon Bonaparte, intent on ruling Europe, invaded the country. As French troops advanced, Adams heard news of continuing troubles in the United States. In light of the unabated harassment of its ships, in June of that same year the United States formally declared war against Britain, signaling the beginning of what came to be known as the War of 1812. With England and Russia allies, Adams worked hard to make sure that the czar understood America's point of view.

But Alexander I had his own problems. As the French army advanced, prospects for his country were looking grim. In September Russians set fire to their own city of Moscow in hopes of denying the French army needed supplies. The plan worked. Though Napoléon was momentarily triumphant, the freezing winter soon gave him no choice but to retreat.

Back in the United States, following initial setbacks that included British troops burning the White House to the ground, the British were finally pushed back. In the spring of 1814 Adams received another message from President Madison. He was asked to negotiate peace with England.

Though America eventually pulled out a victory in the War of 1812, Britain managed to burn the White House and Capitol on August 24, 1814.

The Treaty of Ghent

That June Adams arrived in Ghent, the city in Belgium where the peace talks would be held. Soon he was joined by the other members of the American delegation—James Bayard and Albert Gallatin, along with Henry Clay, speaker of the U.S. House of Representatives, and Jonathan Russell, the U.S. minister to Sweden. Adams was excited to get started, writing, "This opens upon me a . . . new change in the scenery of life. . . . Life in all its forms, high and low, has great, numerous, and exquisite enjoyments."

Despite his high spirits, Adams had to accept that he and his fellow American negotiators had very different temperaments.

Yes, he was America's most experienced diplomat, but now in his late forties, he had become even more argumentative. "My natural disposition," he wrote to Louisa, "is of an over-anxious cast, and my struggles to accommodate myself to circumstances which I cannot control have given my constitution in less than fifty years the wear and tear of seventy."

While Adams liked to eat alone and retire early, his American colleagues stayed up late. He was once famously woken up at 4 AM by one of Clay's drunken card games. Often, Adams grew frustrated to find his initial drafts of documents rewritten by the members of his own committee. Adams was also irritated by their "overbearing insolence," or rudeness, as well as their "narrow understandings" of the issues at hand.

As negotiations began, British forces still occupied eastern Maine and Fort Niagara. Further, England's American Indian allies controlled portions of the Great Lakes and the Mississippi River. Accordingly, England asked for an American Indian buffer state between the United States and Canada, which would deprive the United States of the opportunity for future expansion. British diplomats also angled for control of a portion of the Great Lakes themselves and parts of Maine. Led by Adams, the American diplomats rejected the British terms out of hand. Negotiations were at a standstill.

Soon enough, American victories on the battlefield caused the British to tone down their demands. Though many in England still felt entitled to control parts of the New World, the Duke of Wellington, conqueror of Napoléon, warned his countrymen that the United States could not be invaded without control of the Great Lakes. To win there would exact a heavy toll on British troops.

Weary from its twenty-year clash with France, England eventually agreed to terms that amounted to a truce. In the end the United States gave up no land and lost no land. On Christmas Eve 1814 the Treaty of Ghent was signed.

Unfortunately, in the time it took for word to travel across the Atlantic to the United States, hostilities between the British and Americans continued. Notably, on January 8, 1815, American troops defeated the British in the Battle of New Orleans, turning the winning General Andrew Jackson into a national hero.

After leaving Ghent, Adams traveled to Paris, where he got reacquainted with the city he knew as a boy. In May 1815 President Madison named him America's minister to Great Britain. Serving in England, the Adams family was reunited, as the two oldest boys, George and John, were finally able to make the trip across the Atlantic.

Along with his diplomatic duties, Adams also made time for reading books and writing. "Could I have chosen my own genius and condition," he wrote, "I should have made myself a great poet." That year Adams wrote many poems, often staying up late at night to work on a piece of verse. He wrote, "This evening after retiring to bed nearly at midnight, my thoughts were involuntarily worrying for a rhyme til sleep threatened to jilt me for the night."

Adams was soon taken away from the world of literature and thrust back into the thick of politics. In November 1816 James Monroe was elected the fifth president of the United States and picked Adams to be his secretary of state. It was, as Adams wrote, "A trust of weight and magnitude." On June 10

PEACE !

reaty of PEACE signed & arrived

CENTINEL-OFFICE, *Feb.* 13, 8 o'clock in the morning

ave this instant received in Thirty-two hours from N. York, the follow

Great and Happy News !

ENJAMIN RUSSELL, *Esq. Centinel-Office, Boston,*
New-York, Feb. 11, 1815.—*Saturday Evening,* 10 o'clo

IR—

I HASTEN to acquaint you, for the information of the Public, of
l here this afternoon of H. Br. Majesty's Sloop of War FAVORITE
a has come passenger Mr. CARROLL American Messenger, having in
ssion a

TREATY OF PEACE

en this Country and Great-Britain, signed on the 26th December last.
r. BAKER also is on board, as Agent for the British Government,
who was formerly Charge de Affairs here.
. Carroll reached town at eight o'clock this evening. He shewed t
of mine who is acquainted with him, the pacquet containing the Tre
London Newspaper of the last date of December, announcing the sig
e *Treaty.*

lepends, however, as my friend observed, upon the act of the Presiden
nd hostilities on this side.

e gentlemen left London the 2d Jan. The *Transit* had sailed previo
a port on the Continent.

is city is in a perfect uproar of joy, shouts, illuminations, &c. &c.

ave undertaken to send you this by Express—the rider engaging to deliver it by
k on Monday morning. The expense will be 225 dollars—If you can collect so
emnify me I will thank you so to d

am with respect, Sir, your obedient servant,

JONATHAN GOODHUE

inted at the Portsmouth Oracle-Office.

One of John Quincy Adams' many diplomatic triumphs was successfully helping to negotiate the Treaty of Ghent.

John Quincy Adams as Marksman

While serving as America's ambassador to England, Adams thought he'd show his two older boys how to fire a gun. Unfortunately, he failed to notice that his pistol already carried a charge of powder and added a second. When he fired, the pistol caught on fire and flew a distance of ten feet, leaving his hand burned and his eye badly damaged. It took weeks for his eye to heal.

the following year he continued in his diary, "I bid London adieu, probably forever." On June 15 the family set sail for the United States.

SECRETARY OF STATE *Four*

*J*ohn Quincy Adams arrived back in the United States in 1817 to find a different country than the one he had left in 1809. By opposing the War of 1812 so strongly, the Federalist Party had lost the country's respect. In 1816 James Monroe crushed Rufus King, the last Federalist candidate to run for president, by a margin of 183 electoral votes to 34. After moving into the White House, President Monroe set off on a goodwill tour of the United States, receiving warm ovations from New England to Detroit to Niagara Falls. One reporter announced that an "Era of Good Feelings" had arrived in the country, a phrase that has been used to describe Monroe's eight years in office.

True, the country was finally at peace, its borders secure. But that didn't mean there weren't many important issues to be debated and decided both at home and abroad. Adams found much to keep him busy during his eight years overseeing America's foreign affairs. In fact, many historians count him as the best secretary of state in the nation's history.

TROUBLE WITH FLORIDA

Upon taking office, Adams was faced with the problem of Florida. The western part of the state had been owned by the United States since 1813. But eastern Florida was controlled by Spain, whose government was encouraging local Seminole Indians to attack settlers in bordering Georgia. In 1818 President Monroe authorized General Andrew Jackson, the hero of the Battle of New Orleans, to invade the Spanish territory. Jackson's Tennessee

Future president Andrew Jackson with his troops during the invasion of Pensacola, Florida, in 1818.

militia burned Seminole villages, took several Spanish forts, and killed two British citizens said to be stirring up the Seminoles against the United States. To top it off, he appointed one of his colonels as the state's governor.

Spain's representative to the United States, Luis de Onís y Gonzales-Vara, was furious. He felt that Jackson had gone too far. Many members of the Monroe administration agreed. Yes, the United States wanted to gain control of Florida, but not by brute force. But when President Monroe and his cabinet met to discuss how to apologize to the Spanish government, Adams spoke up in support of Jackson, arguing that the general's actions were justified by the behavior of the Spanish officers in Florida. America's frontiers could not be protected while the Seminoles had a safe haven from which to attack.

Realizing that the American public agreed with Adams, President Monroe decided not to apologize to Spain but to give Adams free reign to negotiate a settlement. Adams went on the offensive, firing off an angry letter to the Spanish government. Jackson was acting from "purest patriotism," he wrote, "acting in the first law of nature, self defense." Further, Spain was too weak to control its possessions. Why else had the country allowed British subjects to rile up Seminoles against peaceful Americans? Adams also chided Britain for allowing its subjects to incite Indian violence.

EUROPEANS IN WASHINGTON

When John Quincy and Louisa Adams moved to Washington, D.C., they found a city that hadn't changed significantly since the last time they lived there. The streets were still covered with mud. Once, on their way to an engagement, the couple's carriage tipped over, compelling Adams to comment, "It was a mercy that we all got home with whole bones."

Because John Quincy and Louisa were accustomed to socializing with Europe's finest, including czars and princes, many Washingtonians found the Adamses to be haughty. John Quincy's Russian hat and coat were subject to special ridicule. Finally, the Adamses took matters into their own hands. In an effort to improve their reputation, in January 1818 they threw a giant ball for three hundred guests. The party was a triumph. From then on John Quincy and Louisa hosted some of the city's most talked about social events.

In the end Adams's letter worked wonders. England quickly decided that the last thing it wanted was another war. And Spain, with its hands full with its colonies in Latin America, decided to negotiate. In 1819 Adams and Onís signed the Transcontinental Treaty (also known as the Adams-Onís Treaty) that gave the United States all of Florida for the relatively low price of $5 million. It also firmed up the border between the United States and Mexico all the way to the Pacific Ocean. Adams rightfully thought of it as one of the great triumphs of his career.

The Missouri Compromise

Undoubtedly, the issue that most sorely divided the country in its first decades was slavery. From the beginning Adams was opposed to the so-called peculiar institution and would spend the

The issue of slavery, which John Quincy Adams was opposed to, was a much heated debate during America's early years.

last years of his career actively fighting against its expansion. Eventually, disagreements between the North, whose residents generally opposed slavery, and the South, whose residents favored it, would lead the country to civil war. Until then lawmakers hammered out a series of compromises between the two regions to keep the peace.

In 1820 the United States faced a crisis having to do with the lands acquired in the Louisiana Purchase. In 1819 the Territory of Missouri petitioned Congress to be admitted to the Union as a slave state. In response the northern-leaning House of Representatives quickly passed the Tallmadge Amendment, a law the stated that no more slaves could be brought into Missouri and provided for the **emancipation** of children born to enslaved parents who were already there. Though the amendment was defeated in the Senate, Southerners were still furious. When the Constitution was adopted in 1788, the North and South were equally wealthy. But in the subsequent thirty-two years northern manufacturing far outearned southern farming. As the North became wealthier and more populated, it gained an advantage over the South in the House of Representatives. But in the Senate, with eleven free states and eleven slave states, representation remained equal. The slave states were determined to keep it that way. After all, if Congress was allowed to outlaw slavery in Missouri, what would stop it from outlawing it in the rest of the South?

As tensions rose, Henry Clay, Adams's negotiating partner from the Treaty of Ghent, then the speaker of the House of Representatives, came up with a compromise. Missouri would be admitted to the Union as a slave state. In order to keep the

One of American history's most influential senators, Henry Clay, served as John Quincy Adams' Secretary of State. He ran unsuccessfully for president three times.

balance of power in the Senate equal, Maine would be admitted as a free state. Further, slavery would not be allowed in the remainder of the Louisiana Purchase above the line of 36° 30', the southern boundary of Missouri.

While most Americans breathed a sign of relief, John Quincy Adams was disgusted, calling slavery's defenders "morally and politically vicious." To him the peculiar institution was an "outrage upon the goodness of God." As the secretary of state, whose charge was foreign affairs, he could not get actively involved in a domestic debate. However, Adams hoped that the compromise might preserve the Union until the North found the political will to outlaw slavery.

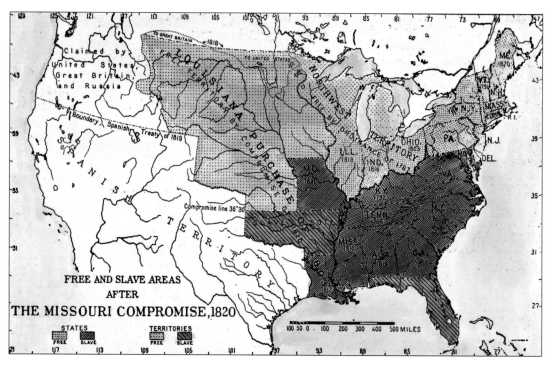

A map of the United States indicating free and slave states following the Missouri Compromise.

THE MONROE DOCTRINE

As secretary of state, Adams saved his best for last. In the early 1820s most of Spain's colonies in Latin America declared their independence. Though the United States was quick to recognize the new countries, France and Russia made motions to support Spain's claims over its former colonies. But Britain was enjoying profitable trade with the newly independent Latin nations. In August 1823 the British foreign secretary, George Canning, approached his American counterpart with a proposition. The United States and England would issue a joint proclamation warning all European nations to stay away from the newly formed Latin republics. Unsure what to do, the American minister reported back to Washington.

Again, Adams stood alone. Many members of the Monroe administration—including ex-presidents Jefferson and Madison—pushed for joining Britain. After all, Great Britain still had the largest and most powerful navy in the world. But Adams thought differently. Wouldn't forming an alliance with Great Britain hamper American expansion? And wouldn't British ships fight to keep trade routes to Latin America open whether they were in league with the United States or not?

During two cabinet meetings on November 7 and 21, 1823, Adams argued forcefully that the United States should act alone. In one of the most famous passages from his diary he summed up his arguments: "It would be more candid," he wrote, "to avow our principles explicitly to Russia and France, than to come in as a cock-boat in the wake of the British man-of-war."

In the end President Monroe sided with Adams. On December 2, 1823, the president added what has become known as the Monroe Doctrine to his annual statement to Congress. From that point forward European countries were not to set up colonies in the Western Hemisphere. They were also warned against interfering with the independence of the newly formed Latin American nations. In return the United States promised to keep its hands off European colonies and not to interfere in the internal affairs of European countries.

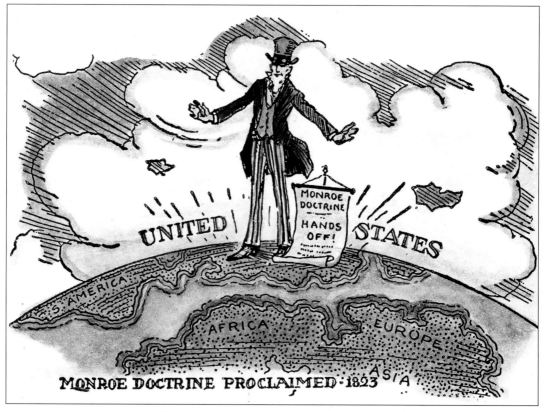

Introduced on December 2, 1823, the Monroe Doctrine, largely formulated and written by John Quincy Adams, stated that any attempts to further colonize the Americas would be viewed as an act of aggression against the United States.

The Monroe Doctrine was one of Adams's shining moments, guiding American foreign policy for years to come. Though justifiably proud of his accomplishment, Adams, ever critical, rounded out his years in the state department unhappy that he hadn't been able to achieve his highest aspiration for the country: a worldwide peace treaty. If he could have done that, he wrote he would "die for it with joy [and] go before the throne on omnipotence with a plea for mercy and with a consciousness of not having lived in vain for the world of mankind."

Running for the White House

With his impressive resume, famous family name, and success as secretary of state, Adams soon became a leading candidate to replace Monroe as president in 1824. Of course, the ever doubtful Adams claimed mixed feelings about trying for the nation's highest office, telling Louisa that politics caused most men to lose their moral bearing. Besides, there were plenty of other men angling for the job: the war hero Andrew Jackson, Speaker of the House Henry Clay, Secretary of the Treasury William Crawford, and the senator from South Carolina John Calhoun. But when Calhoun dropped out to run for the vice presidency, the field narrowed. Soon Adams threw his hat into the ring. By that time his political opponents were already slinging mud, trying to portray Adams in the worst possible light. He complained that "every liar . . . in the country was at work day and night to destroy my character."

In truth the election of 1824 demonstrated how **sectional** loyalties trumped political party. By that time all the leading candidates, including Adams, were aligned with Jefferson's party, at that point called the Democratic-Republican Party.

This political cartoon from 1824 showed that year's presidential candidates John Quincy Adams, William Crawford, and Andrew Jackson lining up to race for the White House. At right, Henry Clay, also a candidate, scratches his head.

Adams became the candidate of New England; Jackson and Clay were the candidates from the South and West. With little dividing them on issues, the campaign turned ugly. Adams was lambasted for having an English wife. Jackson was called a murderer. Clay was called a drunk. In August Adams counted fifteen newspapers around the country whose main objective was to blacken his reputation.

In November 1824 Americans went to the polls to vote for the presidential electors who would then vote for the president. When the votes were counted, none of the four candidates had enough electoral votes to win the presidency outright. (Though ill, William Crawford came in third.)

With no candidate receiving a clear majority, the Constitution called for the election to be decided by the House of Representatives. In last place, Henry Clay realized that he had the power to swing the election. But to whom? Despite differences in temperament, Clay and Adams shared a mutual respect forged at the negotiations of the Treaty of Ghent. The two men also agreed that a high **tariff** on imported goods be instituted and federal support given for internal improvements such as roads and canals. As for Jackson, Clay had never really liked him. He also had no desire to throw the presidency to a fellow westerner. Soon Adams grew more hopeful, observing, "Until recently I had not expected it would be necessary for me to anticipate the event of my election as one for which it would be proper for me even to be prepared."

A Very Close Call

When Adams was elected president by the House of Representatives, the vote could not have been closer. Needing thirteen states to be declared the victor, Adams had twelve locked down. The deciding vote belonged to New York, whose delegation was divided. New York representative General Stephen Van Rensselaer couldn't decide whether to cast his vote for Crawford or Adams. When it was his turn to cast his ballot, he bowed his head to look for divine guidance. On the floor he saw an Adams ballot. Taking it as a sign, Van Rensselaer voted for Adams and handed him the presidency.

When the House met on February 9, 1825, to put the matter to a vote, Adams retired to the State Department. Soon an aide burst into his office with the good news. The House had taken only one ballot. To his surprise, John Quincy Adams had been elected the sixth president of the United States.

PRESIDENT ADAMS

As Adams waited for the fate of the 1824 election to be decided, his feelings were decidedly mixed. In part, he was glad to have proved himself truly worthy of the Adams family name by equaling the position attained by his father. On the other hand, he knew that reaching the White House with barely one-third of the popular vote—becoming a "minority president"—made it very difficult to rule effectively. When granted the high office, he spoke of wishing that the American public could be given the chance to vote again. Since that was impossible, he wrote, "I shall therefore repair to the post assigned me by the call of my country . . . oppressed with the magnitude of the task before me."

Adams didn't sleep for two successive nights before taking office. In his inaugural address he began with a plea for tolerance:

> I am deeply conscious of the prospect that I shall stand more and oftener in need of your indulgence. Intentions upright and pure, a heart devoted to the welfare of our country, and the unceasing application of all the faculties allotted to me to her service are all the pledges that I can give for the faithful performance of the arduous duties I am to undertake.

Adams then made sure to promise a continuation of programs of James Monroe, his very popular predecessor. He fervently hoped that by "friendly, patient, and persevering deliberation all constitutional objections . . . [would] ultimately be removed."

This portrait of John Quincy Adams was completed one year prior to him taking office.

Upon taking office, Adams turned to staffing the government. In past administrations jobs were given to party favorites regardless of talent, a practice known as the spoils system. Determined to keep the best people in government, Adams retained many members of the Monroe administration, even asking William Crawford to stay on as secretary of the treasury. More surprisingly, he offered Andrew Jackson the post of secretary of war. Both refused.

A bad situation got worse when Adams named Henry Clay as his secretary of state. That the two men had a long history and that Clay was qualified for the job didn't matter. In an era when secretary of state was seen as a direct stepping stone to the presidency, Jackson supporters cried that the two men had entered into a "corrupt bargain" in which Clay had handed Adams his electoral votes in exchange for a promise to be the nation's head diplomat. In his diary Adams wrote that Clay did indeed visit him before he took office but was careful to clarify that "He wished me, as far as I might think proper, to satisfy him with regard to some principles of great public importance, but without any personal considerations for himself."

Despite Adams's and Clay's fervent denials that they had struck any sort of deal, Andrew Jackson and his supporters remained unconvinced. A committee to organize the general's presidential campaign for 1828 was formed in Nashville, Tennessee, in 1825. Eight days later Jackson accepted the unofficial nomination. Soon thereafter, he quit the Senate and in effect spent the next four years running for the seat he thought he had been unfairly denied. Meanwhile, his supporters in Congress did whatever they could to block any legislation Adams proposed.

With so much working against him, Adams didn't have much of a chance to be a great or even a good president. He had been a politician who was more admired than liked. Though brilliant, Adams lacked the likeability that might have helped him convince Jackson's supporters to give him a fair chance. So while he is remembered as one of America's most brilliant public servants, John Quincy Adams is ranked as one of the nation's weaker chief executives.

Even so, many great issues of the day commanded his attention. Adams dutifully did his best to do what he thought was right for the country.

The Push for Internal Improvements

John Quincy Adams initially had been unsure of his desire to be president, but once elected, he had firm ideas about what he wanted to do. His main goal was to use his years in office to initiate a program of public works. In his first annual message to Congress, Adams proposed that the federal government fund the construction of a series of roads and canals. He declared that Congress had the duty to promote science and called for the founding of a national university. Pointing out that foreign nations were "advancing with gigantic strides in the career of public improvement," Adams asked for support for an astronomical observatory, a "lighthouse to the sky" where full-time staff would be "in constant attendance of observation upon the phenomena of the heavens."

In hindsight, much of Adams's plan had great validity. In order to take its place alongside its European rivals as a leading industrial nation, the United States needed new infrastructure—

Life in the White House

In the White House Adams was a man of routines. In his era presidents did not have a large Secret Service detail, as they do today. Washington was still a small, unkempt town more than a thriving city. Rising every morning at 5 AM, Adams started his day with a five-mile walk by himself through the countryside. In the summer he often skinny-dipped in the Potomac River. A story goes that a well-known journalist, Anne Royall, once waited by the shore for an interview. When Adams asked her to turn away so he could get dressed, she sat on his clothes until he agreed to answer her questions. Another time Adams and an aide crossed the mighty river in a leaky boat that promptly filled with water. While his companion was able to swim to safety, Adams found it hard to swim in his shirt and pants and nearly drowned. Luckily, he managed to reach land, where he hid behind a rock while his aide went to fetch him a new outfit.

After his morning exercise Adams generally returned to the White House, where he read the Bible and newspapers, ate breakfast, then met with visitors. In the mid–1820s anyone willing to wait his or her turn was able to get an audience with the president of the United States. Dinner was served at five in the afternoon. At night Adams often worked in his chamber by kerosene lamp, going over paperwork, often with the help of his son John, who served as his personal secretary.

roads, canals, and bridges. But Adams's nationalistic views were out of step with those of many voters, who favored government on a state level. Add to the mix the determination of Jackson's supporters to shoot down anything the new president had to propose whether they agreed with it or not, and it becomes clear that Adams's hope for federally funded internal improvements never stood a chance.

Many poor Americans—usually Jackson supporters—felt that projects such as observatories were a waste of money. Southern states—again aligned with Andrew Jackson—worried that a strong federal government would raise tariffs and might even try to abolish slavery. Americans from the South and West also disapproved of Adams's proposed method of paying for the improvements by increasing revenue from the sale of public lands. Westerners, in particular, were upset. After all, if the government increased the price of land, how could poor farmers afford to start their own homesteads? Was the president trying to weaken western states at the expense of the East?

When Adams had first shared his ideas with his cabinet, many of his department heads expressed reservations. William Wirt, the attorney general and Adams's good friend, found the message "excessively bold." After Adams described his vision in a speech, newspapers around the country ridiculed much of the plan, especially his call for national observatories.

The alliance of Jackson, Crawford, and Calhoun's voters defeated all of Adams's scientific and educational proposals, as well as his plans to build new roads and canals. Worse, Adams's proposals to strengthen the Bank of the United States and to refinance the public debt were also defeated. Adams wrote, "I fell, and with me fell, I fear never to rise again . . . in my day, the system of internal improvements by means of national energies. The great object of my life . . . has failed."

The Erie Canal

Though Adams's wide-ranging agenda of internal improvements failed to pass in Congress, one of America's greatest industrial projects was completed while Adams was in office. In 1817 work had begun on the Erie Canal, a man-made waterway that ran from New York State's capitol, Albany, to Buffalo and Lake Erie. Though a trip down the canal's approximately 360 miles took four and a half days, the completion of the Erie Canal marked an enormous change in the early American economy. With the canal operational, goods could be shipped between Buffalo and New York City for one-tenth the cost of moving them overland.

The Tariff of Abominations

Tariffs on goods shipped to the United States from foreign countries was an issue that split the country during Adams's presidency. Often, British goods cost less than those manufactured in America. As a result New England businesses looked to stay competitive by lobbying for high tariffs on imported British goods. While this policy helped the manufacturers in New England, it hurt the South by forcing southerners to pay higher prices for goods that weren't produced in their states. President Monroe had increased the so-called protective tariff in 1816 from its general level of

This issue of tariffs on imports to the United States split North/South relations during John Quincy Adams' presidency.

20 to 25 percent to about 37 percent. But some New England manufacturers wanted the rates to go even higher.

As president, Adams proposed a "cautious" approach to the tariff issue, maintaining "tender and sincere regard to the agricultural interest of the South and the commercial interest of the North."

But Jackson's supporters were not interested in passing a bill that looked out for the best interests of both regions. Rather, they were interested in finding another way to embarrass the president. Even though many of Jackson's supporters were from the South and favored lower tariff rates, southern congressmen pushed through a bill that raised the tariff an astonishing 45 percent, even on goods that were desperately needed by New England manufacturers, such as wool. The Jacksonites figured that the New England congressmen would have to vote against a bill that so heavily taxed items needed by their home region. Instead, the congressmen from the North, who believed in protecting their industries, held their noses and voted for the bill, passing it into law.

Despite playing a large part in passing a bill that nobody wanted, southerners instantly objected. They called the new tariff "The Black Tariff" or "The Tariff of Abominations," pointing out that the "Yankee tariff" discriminated against them. After all, the rest of the world's countries traded goods in a free market that was unprotected by tariffs. Meanwhile, southerners were forced to buy their goods in American markets, where tariffs drove prices higher. In South Carolina people were so angry that some flags were lowered to half mast. On the other hand, some southerners failed to realize that a prosperous Northeast was in their best interest. When northerners were doing well, they could buy southerners' cotton and farm produce.

John Calhoun and Nullification

John Calhoun was one of the most prominent senators of his day. Hailing from South Carolina, he was a candidate for president in 1824 until he stepped down to run for vice president. In those days the president and his vice president didn't necessarily share the same views. So it was with Adams and Calhoun. When the Tariff of Abominations became law, Calhoun penned a pamphlet called "The South Carolina Exposition and Protest." In it Calhoun argued that states could ignore, or nullify, federal laws with which they disagreed. When no other state joined South Carolina in its fervent anti-tariff stance, Calhoun's paper was quietly shelved—for the time being. In truth, while Calhoun was trying to find a way for southern states to coexist with the North, his idea of nullification of federal laws was the first step toward southerners claiming the right to secede from the Union altogether, which led to the Civil War in 1860.

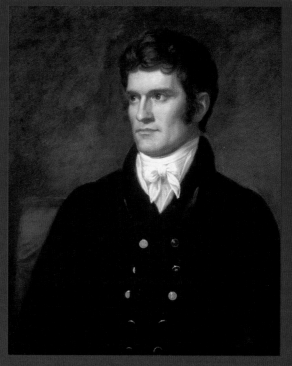

Adams and Foreign Affairs

If Adams had trouble convincing Congress to pass his bill of internal improvements, foreign affairs was an area where he would be expected to succeed. Hadn't he negotiated the Treaty of Ghent? Wasn't he the man who had wrested Florida from Spain for only $5 million? Wasn't he the author of the brilliant Monroe Doctrine?

Ironically, while Adams is rightfully remembered as one of the best statesmen in American history, it is not for deeds done during his time in the White House. After besting the British diplomatically throughout his career, the English foreign minister finally returned the favor. Since America's founding in 1776, trade with the British West Indies had been either closed or subject to severe restrictions. In 1826 Adams made an awkward attempt to open West Indies trade to American ships; London said no.

Adams also ran into trouble in Panama. In 1826 Simón Bolívar, a hero of the South American wars of independence, called for a Panama Congress to discuss issues pertaining to the region. Bolívar invited the United States to attend. Secretary of State Clay eagerly accepted, and Adams appointed two delegates. Then he unwisely asked the Senate for its approval. Supporters of Jackson rose to criticize America's relations with South America. Though Adams finally won the approval he needed, it was too late. One of his chosen delegates died en route to the conference, and the other arrived after it was over. His foes viewed it as another golden opportunity to shower Adams with ridicule.

The Election of 1828

No fool, Adams knew that his days in the White House were numbered well before he ran for reelection. After the death of his father, he noted that he'd need a place to live "within two or three years" for "a place of retirement." By 1827 he found his presidential duties so stressful that he suffered from insomnia and indigestion. He was keenly aware that he wasn't a natural politician who felt at ease with the masses. After the dedication of the Chesapeake and Ohio Canal, he wrote in his diary, "As has happened to me whenever I have had a part to perform in the presence of multitudes, I got through awkwardly, but without gross and palpable failure."

The 1828 campaign began where the 1824 campaign had left off. With the demise of the Federalists, the United States had split into two new political parties. Adams was now head of the National Republicans. Andrew Jackson ran under the flag of the Democratic-Republicans, soon shortened simply to the Democrats. From the beginning Jackson and his supporters

The Adams Difference

In 1829 Louisa Adams wrote one of her sons, explaining what made the Adams family stand apart from the rest: "Our tastes, our tempers, our habits vary so much from those of the herd that we can never be beloved or admired, but we may and must be respected—unless we forget the respect we owe ourselves."

decried the "corrupt bargain," doing everything they could to portray Adams, perhaps one of the most upstanding men ever to occupy the White House, as dishonest. While Jackson was heralded as a man of the people, Adams was derided for his "dandy dress of nankeen pantaloons and silk stockings" and was falsely accused of buying a billiard table for the White House with government money.

In truth, Adams's supporters were just as harsh. As Adams wrote, "In the excitement of contested elections . . . [m]en of intelligence, talents, and even of integrity upon other occasions, surrender themselves up to their passions." Most notably, Adams's

This political cartoon shows John Quincy clinging to the presidential chair with Henry Clay behind him. Both men are on the back of John Binns, a well-known newspaper editor, who is burdened by the coffins he had used to illustrate an anti-Jackson handbill.

supporters accused Jackson of adultery when he unknowingly married his wife, Rachel, before her divorce was official. One piece of campaign literature read, "Ought a convicted adulteress and her paramour husband be placed in the highest offices of this free and Christian land?"

In the end Jackson's supporters were better organized and more motivated. As one Adams voter put it, the Jacksonians were "swimming rivers and risking their lives to get to the polls." Adams's partisans, on the other hand, generally supported their candidate more out of a sense of duty than any real enthusiasm. Accordingly, on election day, the people handed down the verdict that Adams had been expecting. Jackson won easily, with 178 electoral votes to Adams's 83.

Adams gave a final speech to Congress to extol what he had accomplished, noting that the United States now enjoyed free trade throughout the Western Hemisphere, with the exception of England. He pointed to advances in naval preparedness and officer training. He also mentioned that under his leadership, the United States had become more prosperous. The public revenue had increased by $18 million; $30 million of its debt had been paid down.

Though Adams was happy to leave office, it was not without bitterness. On inauguration day he refused to stay to listen to Jackson's speech. For his part, Jackson wouldn't visit Adams in the White House before taking office. Though she had lived to see her husband win the presidency, Rachel Jackson had died before he could be sworn in. Jackson attributed his wife's failing health and eventual death to the strain she felt upon hearing continuing charges of adultery during the campaign trail. He never forgave Adams or his supporters.

Andrew Jackson was the first American president to come from humble origins and not attend college.

Peacefield or "Old House," was John Quincy's home in Quincy, Massachusetts.

After Andrew Jackson took over the reins of government, Adams returned to the family home in Quincy, Massachusetts. Fully expecting to retire from politics, he wrote, "The sun of my political life sets in the deepest gloom."

THE DEATH OF TWO LEGENDS

Midway through John Quincy Adams's term, his thoughts turned to his father. As the nation celebrated its fiftieth birthday, on July 4, 1826, John Adams, ninety-one years old, was near death at his home in Braintree. By astonishing coincidence Thomas Jefferson, age eighty-three, was also failing rapidly on the same day. Thomas Jefferson died a few hours before Adams at his estate in Monticello in Virginia.

The Final Act: Congressman Adams

*T*hroughout his career John Quincy Adams proved himself able to negotiate with kings and presidents. But by his own admission he sometimes had trouble dealing with the people in his life with the same sensitivity. Adams's relationship with his two eldest sons, George and John, was particularly strained. Though neither boy was especially studious, Adams held them to the same high standards to which his father had held him. But where Adams responded to his father's entreaties, George and John did not. During his presidency, Adams grew so upset with young John's performance at Harvard that he forbade him from visiting Washington over Christmas unless his class rank rose to the top five. When young John wrote, asking his father to change his mind, Adams refused, writing his son, "I would feel nothing but sorrow and shame in your presence."

But it was Adams's eldest son, George, who would suffer the most. As he grew older, George began to gamble and drink. Toward the end of Adams's term in the White House his third son, Charles, wrote to say that George was severely troubled. Adams asked George to come to Washington to help him and Louisa pack for their return to Quincy. While riding on a steamboat to meet his parents, George Adams was reported to appear disturbed. An hour before sunrise he walked to the deck and spoke briefly with another passenger. After that he disappeared, leaving only his hat lying on the deck. His body washed up on a nearby beach two weeks later.

Adams was devastated at the news and chided himself for pushing George too hard. Adams wrote, "The afflictions with which we [Adams and Louisa] have visited . . . have so weakened us in body and mind that our dejection of spirits seems irrecoverable." While mourning his son, Adams also learned that he had lost much of his money in a bad business venture. Small wonder that Adams referred to 1829 as his "furnace of affliction."

Congressman Adams

After George's death Adams found solace in gardening and reading. September 1830 brought the happy arrival of a second granddaughter, Fanny. On the seventeenth of that month Adams felt well enough to attend a celebration of the two-hundredth anniversary of Boston's founding. Also at the festivities were two longtime supporters, the newspaper editor John B. Davis and the Quincy congressman Reverend Joseph Richardson. The two men called on Adams the next day at his home and asked if he would be willing to run for Congress.

It was a most unusual proposal. Until that time the typical course for ex-presidents was to retire to a quiet life and rarely speak out about politics. But Adams was intrigued, avowing that if the people called on him, he might serve. Adams's family, however, was firmly against it. Now happily settled in Quincy, Louisa stated that she refused to ever move back to Washington. His youngest son, Charles, felt to serve in Congress after being president was undignified. Even so, Adams let it be known that while he would not formally campaign, he would not refuse the office if elected. On November 7 he won

John Quincy Adams still remains the only president to return to public life in a lower office.

BANKRUPT

Following his years in the White House Adams found himself in financial difficulties. Along with a series of bad investments, tragedy struck again when his second son, John, died at age thirty-one, leaving behind a wife and two daughters who Adams felt obligated to care for. John had also left behind $15,000 in debts. "You must understand," Adams told his lone surviving son, Charles, "that there is now here little else than debts." Luckily, Charles turned out to be the responsible son Adams had always hoped for. Charles promptly told his father that he must spend less and sell off some of the family property, saying how he wished "that your mind should be put at ease at once from the anxiety which I know has been preying upon it for years." After some heated arguments Adams finally agreed and lived without undue financial strain for the rest of his life.

75 percent of the vote. A few months earlier the loss of the White House and the death of his son had left him bereft. His election to Congress was rejuvenating.

THE GAG RULE

On December 5, 1831, Adams took his seat in the House of Representatives. For the next seventeen years he became one of the most outspoken, successful congressmen of his era. In 1836 Louisa expressed her husband's most fervent hopes for the tail end of his career, "[T]hat he may leave a fame to posterity and awaken the justice of this nation to record his name as one of the fairest midst the race of man." It is safe to say that Adams lived up to his wife's wishes.

The issue that Adams pitted himself against with great passion was slavery. The Missouri Compromise of 1820 had temporarily eased tensions between the North and the South. But in the 1830s the movement to abolish slavery in the United States was gaining traction in the North. Adams soon became the leading spokesman in Congress for the rights of men and women in bondage.

Abolitionists tried many tactics to bring home their point. They wrote angry editorials and printed pamphlets that decried the horrors of slavery. Some worked for the Underground Railroad, through which slaves were snuck off their home planta-

By virtue of special compact, Shylock demanded a pound of flesh, cut nearest to the heart. Those who sell mothers separately from their children, likewise claim a legal right to human flesh; and they too cut it nearest to the *heart.—L. M. Child.*

On. woman! from thy happy hearth
Extend thy gentle hand to save
The poor and perishing of earth—
The chained and stricken slave!
Oh, plead for all the suffering of thy kind—
For the crushed body and the darkened
mind.   *J. G. Whittier.*

FIFTH ANNIVERSARY
OF THE
MASSACHUSETTS ANTI-SLAVERY SOCIETY,
WEDNESDAY, JANUARY 25, 1837.

[☞ The public meetings, during the day, will be held in the SPACIOUS LOFT, OVER THE STABLE OF THE MARLBOROUGH HOTEL, and in the evening, in the REPRESENTATIVES' HALL.]

HOURS OF THE MEETINGS.
Meeting for Delegates at 9 o'clock in the morning, at 46, Washington-Street.

First public meeting at 10 o'clock A. M., in the LOFT OVER THE STABLE OF THE MARLBOROUGH HOTEL.

Second public meeting at 1-2 past 2 o'clock, P. M. same place.

Evening meeting at 1-2 past 6 o'clock, in the REPRESENTATIVES' HALL.

☞ The Committee of Arrangements respectfully inform the ladies that ample accommodations have been prepared for them. The loft is spacious, clean, well warmed, and will accommodate, with ease and perfect safety, at least 1000 persons.

☞ AMOS DRESSER, a citizen of this State, who was 'Lynched' at Nashville, for the crime of being an Abolitionist, will be present, and during the meetings in the afternoon and evening, will give a history of that affair.

A notice announcing the meeting of the Massachusetts Anti-Slavery Society, 1837.

tions and brought north to live in freedom. Another ploy used by abolitionists was to send petitions to the House of Representatives to encourage debate on the subject.

Before long Adams became the antislavery movement's point man in Congress. One of his first acts in the House was to present fifteen petitions, each asking Congress to abolish slavery in the District of Columbia. In fact, every Monday for his first years in office, Adams dutifully presented antislavery petitions to the House, infuriating southern Congressmen. Finally, the southern block struck back. In 1836 Representative Henry Laurens Pinckney of South Carolina introduced three resolutions to Congress. The first two stated that Congress had no right to interfere with slavery in either the states or the District of Columbia. The final resolution was the most inflammatory, stating that all future petitions regarding the **abolition** of slavery should be automatically withdrawn "and that no further action whatever shall be had thereon."

The seventy-year-old Adams was outraged. Jumping to his feet, he tried to speak against the first resolution. But the speaker of the House, a southerner, would not recognize him. "Am I gagged?" Adams called. Ignored but not defeated, Adams waited until the third resolution was brought before the House. When called to vote, Adams cried, "I hold the resolution to be in direct violation of the Constitution of the United States, of the rules of this House, and of the rights of my constituents." Despite Adams's objections, the resolution passed by a vote of 117 to 68.

From that day forward Adams's passion became the overturning of the so-called gag rule that limited debate on slavery. Every chance he got the elderly statesman jumped to his feet with the energy of a man half his age to offer new petitions for

A cartoon satarizing the "gag-rule" whereby southern members of the House of Representatives refused to allow discussion on the subject of slavery.

the abolition of slavery. Southerners were furious, and Adams received death threats. One was a picture of him with a bullet hole in his head. Another informed Adams that a lynch mob was coming to Washington to "string him up from the highest oak on the grounds of the national Capitol."

Adams never gave up. Year after year he moved to have the gag rule rescinded. Year after year he lost—but each time the vote got closer and closer. Then on December 3, 1844, Adams tried again. This time his resolution finally passed. Due to Adams's efforts, northern Congressmen were able to once again decry the evils of slavery.

THE *AMISTAD* CASE

In 1839, fifty-two Africans were kidnapped and shipped to Cuba. There they were sold to two Spanish traders who placed them aboard a ship called the *Amistad* for shipment to a sugar plantation to work as slaves. Along the way the Africans rebelled, killing most of the crew. Eventually, the ship ended up in New York Harbor, where the Africans were arrested and charged with murder.

By 1841 the case had reached the Supreme Court. A known expert in international relations, John Quincy Adams was asked to argue the case for the accused Africans. On February 23, 1841, Adams spoke before the court for four hours without notes. A week later he returned and spoke for three more hours, arguing that the Africans should not be considered slaves under international law. Adams went further, insisting that the only true crime committed by the Africans was the same crime committed by the members of the American Revolution: fighting oppressors. On March 9 the Supreme Court ruled that the Africans imprisoned on the *Amistad* could go free.

A Fighter Until the End

John Quincy Adams stayed actively involved in the issues of the day until the very end of his life. Worried about the possible spread of slavery into new territories, he voted against America's involvement in the Mexican War and the annexation of Texas. Having gained the respect of his colleagues, his nickname in the House of Representatives became "Old Man Eloquent." Due in large part to his continuing fight against the expansion of slavery, Adams finally became popular. When he traveled, he was greeted by cheering crowds. After a trip to Niagara Falls in 1843, he was welcomed back into the United States by more than one thousand supporters.

An elderly man, Adams was showing signs of age. On November 20, 1846, he fell while walking on a Boston street. The diagnosis was a minor stroke. After a few months in recovery, he returned to the House of Representatives, where he worked for the next year. Then on February 21, 1848, while

The last picture of John Quincy Adams, a year before his death in 1848.

THE SMITHSONIAN

While Adams was in Congress, a British scientist named James Smithson left the United States $500,000 "for the increase and diffusion of knowledge among men." It was Adams's duty to make sure that the money was well spent. After years of congressional in-fighting, Adams succeeded in earmarking the gift for a free museum in downtown Washington. Today, the Smithsonian Institution is a sprawling complex of fourteen buildings that house museums, art galleries, libraries, and a zoo. It even houses Adams's longed-for observatory.

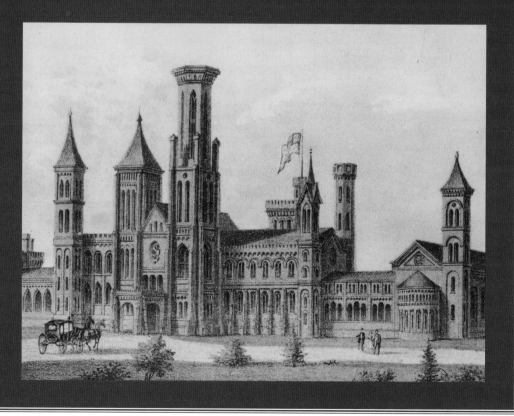

Congress was voting on a treaty to end the war with Mexico, Adams clutched the edge of his desk. His face turned red.

Adams was carried to an adjoining room and laid on a couch. He revived for a few moments and called for his old friend Henry Clay. Later he said, "This is the end of earth, but I am composed." He died two days later.

In the wake of his death John Quincy Adams would have been surprised and most probably very pleased at the outpouring of sentiment from the nation. According to his son Charles, the official tribute to honor his life at the Capitol was "as great a pageant as was ever conducted in the United States," one that demonstrated "the homage of people for a truly worthy public servant." Adams's remains lay in state for two days while thousands of Americans passed by to pay their respects. Americans mourned one of their most talented and committed politicians. Then Adams was taken home to Quincy, Massachusetts, and buried on Penn's Hill, next to his parents.

While his presidency was less than

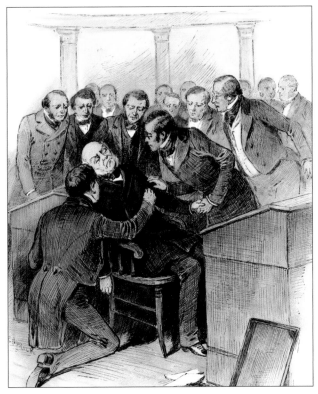

Adams succumbs to a stroke at the House of Representatives.

successful, Adams's brilliant career as a diplomat and secretary of state, topped off by an inspiring fight to stop the expansion of slavery, more than made up for it. His tombstone reads "Born a citizen of Massachusetts. Died a citizen of the United States."

Though the presidency of John Quincy Adams was not as successful as others, his career as a public servant stands out amongst many.

TIMELINE

1767
Born in Braintree, Massachusetts

1781
Named chief aide to Francis Dana, America's diplomat to Russia

1787
Graduates Harvard University second in his class

1794
Named the U.S. ambassador to the Netherlands

1797
Marries Louisa Johnson

1803
Serves as U.S. senator for Massachusetts

1760

1809
Named U.S. ambassador to Russia

1817
Appointed U.S. secretary of state

1825
Becomes America's sixth president

1829
Retires to Quincy, Massachusetts

1830
Elected to Congress, where he serves for seventeen years

1848
Dies at the age of eighty

1850

NOTES

CHAPTER ONE

p. 7, "You come into life . . .": John Adams, quoted in Paul C. Nagel, *John Quincy Adams, A Public Life, A Private Life* (New York: Alfred A. Knopf, 1997), 76.

p. 7, "I am a man of reserved, . . .": John Quincy Adams, quoted in Thomas A. Bailey, *The American Pageant, Volume I,* Fifth Edition (Lexington, MA: D.C. Heath and Company, 1975), 259.

p. 8, "I am forty-five years old . . .": John Quincy Adams, quoted in John F. Kennedy, *Profiles in Courage* (New York: Harper Perennial, 2006), 33.

p. 8, "John Quincy Adams . . . held . . .": Quoted in Kennedy, *Profiles in Courage*, 33.

p. 8, "Above all cares of this life . . .": John Adams, quoted in Nagel, *John Quincy Adams, A Public Life, A Private Life*, 10.

p. 9, ". . . an office so useful to his Mamma . . .": John Adams, quoted in Nagel, *John Quincy Adams, A Public Life, A Private Life*, 7.

p. 12, "I love to receive letters . . .": John Quincy Adams, quoted in Kennedy, *Profiles in Courage*, 32–33.

p. 14, "To describe the ocean . . .": John Adams, quoted in Nagel, *John Quincy Adams, A Public Life, A Private Life*, 13.

p. 14, ". . . fully sensible of our danger . . .": John Adams, quoted in Nagel, *John Quincy Adams, A Public Life, A Private Life*, 13.

p. 15, ". . . learned more French in . . .": John Adams, quoted in Nagel, *John Quincy Adams, A Public Life, A Private Life*, 15.

p. 15, "For dear as you are to me . . .": Abigail Adams, quoted in Nagel, *John Quincy Adams, A Public Life, A Private Life*, 16.

p. 15, "My son gives me great pleasure . . .": John Adams, quoted in Nagel, *John Quincy Adams, A Public Life, A Private Life*, 16.

p. 20, ". . . the greatest traveler of his age . . .": John Adams, quoted in Nagel, *John Quincy Adams, A Public Life, A Private Life*, 33.

CHAPTER TWO

p. 22, "You are admitted, Adams.": Reverend Joseph Willard, quoted in Nagel, *John Quincy Adams, A Public Life, A Private Life*, 44.

p. 22, "[John's] attention to his studies, . . .": Reverend Joseph Willard, quoted in Nagel, *John Quincy Adams, A Public Life, A Private Life*, 53.

p. 24, "I felt a depression of the spirits . . .": John Quincy Adams, quoted in Nagel, *John Quincy Adams, A Public Life, A Private Life*, 60.

p. 25, "On thee thy ardent lover's . . .": John Quincy Adams, quoted in Nagel, *John Quincy Adams, A Public Life, A Private Life*, 65.

p. 25, "Common fame reports that you are attached . . .": Abigail Adams, quoted in Nagel, *John Quincy Adams, A Public Life, A Private Life*, 67.

p. 25, ". . . four years of exquisite wretchedness . . .": John Quincy Adams, quoted in Nagel, *John Quincy Adams, A Public Life, A Private Life*, 69.

p. 29, "I wish I could have been consulted . . .": John Quincy Adams, quoted in Nagel, *John Quincy Adams, A Public Life, A Private Life*, 81.

p. 30, ". . . goodness of heart and gentleness . . .": John Quincy Adams, quoted in Nagel, *John Quincy Adams, A Public Life, A Private Life*, 100.

CHAPTER THREE

p. 35, "Lord! How the Federalists will stare . . .": Quoted in Bailey, *The American Pageant, Volume 1*, Fifth Edition, 189.

p. 39, "Curse on the stripling . . .": Quoted in Kennedy, *Profiles in Courage*, 38.

p. 39, "I do not disapprove of your conduct . . .": John Adams, quoted in Kennedy, *Profiles in Courage*, 38.

p. 39, "I have already had occasion to experience . . .": John Quincy Adams, quoted in Kennedy, *Profiles in Courage*, 38.

p. 40, ". . . a capital of miserable huts . . .": Quoted in Miriam Greenblatt, *John Quincy Adams: 6th President of the United States* (New York: Garrett Educational Corporation, 1990), 31.

p. 42, "This measure will cost . . .": John Quincy Adams, quoted in Kennedy, *Profiles in Courage*, 43.

p. 42, "A party scavenger! . . .": Quoted in Kennedy, *Profiles in Courage*, 44.

p. 42, "I would not sit at the same . . .": Quoted in Kennedy, *Profiles in Courage*, 44.

p. 42, ". . . you have too honest a heart . . .": John Adams, quoted in Kennedy, *Profiles in Courage*, 45.

p. 43, ". . . far from regretting any one . . .": John Quincy Adams, quoted in Kennedy, *Profiles in Courage*, 47.

p. 44, "Make your talents and your knowledge . . .": John Quincy Adams, quoted in Nagel, *John Quincy Adams, A Public Life, A Private Life*, 190.

p. 46, "I am also, and always shall be . . .": John Quincy Adams, quoted in Nagel, *John Quincy Adams, A Public Life, A Private Life*, 199.

p. 48, "I don't like Americans; . . .": Michael Scott, quoted in Bailey, *The American Pageant, Volume 1*, Fifth Edition, 227.

p. 48, "This opens upon me a . . .": John Quincy Adams, quoted in Nagel, *John Quincy Adams, A Public Life, A Private Life*, 215.

p. 49, "My natural disposition . . .": John Quincy Adams, quoted in Nagel, *John Quincy Adams, A Public Life, A Private Life*, 218.

p. 49, ". . . overbearing insolence . . .": John Quincy Adams, quoted in Nagel, *John Quincy Adams, A Public Life, A Private Life*, 219.

p. 50, "Could I have chosen my own genius . . .": John Quincy Adams, quoted in Nagel, *John Quincy Adams, A Public Life, A Private Life*, 231.

p. 50, "This evening after retiring . . .": John Quincy Adams, quoted in Nagel, *John Quincy Adams, A Public Life, A Private Life*, 232.

NOTES

p. 50, "A trust of weight and magnitude . . .": John Quincy Adams, quoted in Nagel, *John Quincy Adams, A Public Life, A Private Life*, 233.

p. 53, "I bid London adieu . . .": John Quincy Adams, quoted in Nagel, *John Quincy Adams, A Public Life, A Private Life*, 235.

CHAPTER FOUR

p. 56, ". . . purest patriotism . . . acting in the first law . . .": John Quincy Adams, quoted in Greenblatt, *John Quincy Adams: 6th President of the United States*, 58.

p. 56, "It was a mercy that we . . .": John Quincy Adams, quoted in Nagel, *John Quincy Adams, A Public Life, A Private Life*, 251.

p. 60, ". . . morally and politically vicious . . .": John Quincy Adams, quoted in Nagel, *John Quincy Adams, A Public Life, A Private Life*, 266.

p. 61, "It would be more candid . . .": John Quincy Adams, quoted in Nagel, *John Quincy Adams, A Public Life, A Private Life*, 270.

p. 63, ". . . die for it with joy . . .": John Quincy Adams, quoted in Nagel, *John Quincy Adams, A Public Life, A Private Life*, 271.

p. 63, ". . . every liar . . . in the country was . . .": John Quincy Adams, quoted in Nagel, *John Quincy Adams, A Public Life, A Private Life*, 289.

p. 65, "Until recently I had not . . .": John Quincy Adams, quoted in Nagel, *John Quincy Adams, A Public Life, A Private Life*, 293.

CHAPTER FIVE

p. 67, "I shall therefore repair . . .": John Quincy Adams, quoted in Nagel, *John Quincy Adams, A Public Life, A Private Life*, 297.

p. 67, "I am deeply conscious of the prospect . . .": John Quincy Adams, quoted in Mary W. M. Hargreaves, *The Presidency of John Quincy Adams* (Lawrence, KS: University of Kansas Press, 1985), 41.

p. 67, ". . . friendly, patient, and persevering . . .": John Quincy Adams, quoted in Hargreaves, *The Presidency of John Quincy Adams*, 42.

p. 69, "He wished me, as far as . . .": John Quincy Adams, quoted in Hargreaves, *The Presidency of John Quincy Adams*, 38.

p. 70, ". . . advancing with gigantic strides . . .": John Quincy Adams, quoted in Nagel, *John Quincy Adams, A Public Life, A Private Life*, 302.

p. 72, ". . . excessively bold . . .": William Wirt, quoted in Nagel, *John Quincy Adams, A Public Life, A Private Life*, 302.

p. 72, "I fell, and with me fell . . .": John Quincy Adams, quoted in Greenblatt, *John Quincy Adams: 6th President of the United States*, 79.

p. 75, ". . . tender and sincere regard to the agricultural . . .": John Quincy Adams, quoted in Nagel, *John Quincy Adams, A Public Life, A Private Life*, 302.

p. 78, ". . . within two or three years . . .": John Quincy Adams, quoted in Hargreaves, *The Presidency of John Quincy Adams*, 253.

p. 78, "As has happened to me whenever . . .": John Quincy Adams, quoted in Hargreaves, *The Presidency of John Quincy Adams*, 255.

p. 78, "Our tastes, our tempers, . . .": Louisa Adams, quoted in Hargreaves, *The Presidency of John Quincy Adams*, 253.

p. 79, "dandy dress of nankeen pantaloons . . .": Quoted in Hargreaves, *The Presidency of John Quincy Adams*, 287.

p. 79, "In the excitement of contested . . .": John Quincy Adams, quoted in Nagel, *John Quincy Adams, A Public Life, A Private Life*, 319.

p. 80, "Ought a convicted adulteress . . .": Quoted in Greenblatt, *John Quincy Adams, 6th President of the United States*, 83.

p. 80, ". . . swimming rivers and risking . . .": Quoted in Hargreaves, *The Presidency of John Quincy Adams*, 298.

p. 82, "The sun of my political life . . .": John Quincy Adams, quoted in Nagel, *John Quincy Adams, A Public Life, A Private Life*, 321.

CHAPTER SIX

p. 83, "I would feel nothing . . .": John Quincy Adams, quoted in Nagel, *John Quincy Adams, A Public Life, A Private Life*, 279.

p. 84, "The afflictions with which we . . .": John Quincy Adams, quoted in Nagel, *John Quincy Adams, A Public Life, A Private Life*, 330.

p. 84, ". . . furnace of affliction . . .": John Quincy Adams, quoted in Greenblatt, *John Quincy Adams: 6th President of the United States*, 86.

p. 86, "You must understand . . .": John Quincy Adams, quoted in Nagel, *John Quincy Adams, A Public Life, A Private Life*, 347.

p. 86, ". . . that your mind should . . .": Charles Adams, quoted in Nagel, *John Quincy Adams, A Public Life, A Private Life*, 348.

p. 86, ". . . that he may leave a fame . . .": Louisa Adams, quoted in Nagel, *John Quincy Adams, A Public Life, A Private Life*, 356.

p. 88, ". . . and that no further action . . .": Henry Laurens Pinckney, quoted in Greenblatt, *John Quincy Adams: 6th President of the United States*, 99.

p. 88, "I hold the resolution . . .": John Quincy Adams, quoted in Greenblatt, *John Quincy Adams: 6th President of the United States*, 101.

p. 89, ". . . string him up from the highest . . .": Quoted in Greenblatt, *John Quincy Adams: 6th President of the United States*, 104.

p. 92, ". . . for the increase and diffusion of . . .": James Smithson, quoted in Greenblatt, *John Quincy Adams: 6th President of the United States*, 91.

p. 93, "This is the end . . .": John Quincy Adams, quoted in Greenblatt, *John Quincy Adams: 6th President of the United States*, 115.

p. 93, ". . . as great a pageant . . .": Charles Adams, quoted in Nagel, *John Quincy Adams, A Public Life, A Private Life*, 414–15.

GLOSSARY

abolition the act or practice of doing away with a system, practice, or institution

apprenticed sent out to learn a trade from a skilled employer

colonists first inhabitants of a colony

constitution a body of fundamental principles according to which a country or organization agrees to be governed

delegates people who are designated to act for or represent others

diplomatic concerning the profession or skill of managing international relations

domestic relating to issues pertaining to one's own country

emancipation the freeing of someone from the control of another

embargo an order of government prohibiting movement of merchant ships into or out of certain ports

exports goods or services for sale to another country

Federalist Party a political party that supported a strong central government

independent standing alone

Jeffersonian-Republicans supporters of the Jeffersonian-Republican Party, which supported states' rights

majority the number greater than half the total

maverick an independent-minded person

nullification the voiding or canceling of a law

partisan a strong supporter of a party, cause, or person

patriot a person who vigorously supports his or her country

resolution a formal expression of opinion or intention agreed on by a legislative body

sectional of or relating to a section of a larger whole

tariffs taxes to be paid on particular exports or imports

FURTHER INFORMATION

BOOKS

Mara, Wil. *John Adams*. New York: Marshall Cavendish Benchmark, 2009.

Marsico, Katie. *Andrew Jackson*. New York: Marshall Cavendish Benchmark, 2010.

Wheelan, Joseph. *Mr. Adams's Last Crusade: John Quincy Adams's Extraordinary Post-Presidential Life in Congress*. New York: Public Affairs, 2008.

WEBSITES

American Presidents: Life Portraits

www.americanpresidents.org/presidents/president.
  asp?PresidentNumber=6

This site on the American presidents offers facts, a biography, and links on John Quincy Adams.

Miller Center of Public Affairs: Essays on John Quincy Adams

http://millercenter.org/academic/americanpresident/jqadams

This site offers essays on John Quincy Adams and his administration.

The White House

www.whitehouse.gov/about/presidents/johnquincyadams/

At the official website of the White House, explore a brief biography of
John Quincy Adams, as well as links to biographies of other presidents.

BIBLIOGRAPHY

Bailey, Thomas A. *The American Pageant: A History of the Republic, Vols. 1–2*, Fifth Edition. Lexington, MA: D.C. Heath and Company, 1975.

Davis, Kenneth C. *Don't Know Much About History*. New York: Avon Books, 1990.

Greenblatt, Miriam. *John Quincy Adams: 6th President of the United States*. Ada, OK: Garrett Educational Corporation, 1990.

Hargreaves, Mary W. M. *The Presidency of John Quincy Adams*. Lawrence, KS: University Press of Kansas, 1985.

Hofstadter, Richard. *Great Issues in American History: From the Revolution to the Civil War, 1765–1865*. New York: Vintage Books, 1958.

Nagel, Paul. C. *John Quincy Adams, A Public Life, A Private Life*. New York: Alfred A. Knopf, 1997.

INDEX

Pages in **boldface** are illustrations.

ABOUT THE AUTHOR

Dan Elish is the author of numerous fiction and history books for children, including *The Trail of Tears*, *Vermont*, *Franklin Delano Roosevelt*, and *Theodore Roosevelt*, for Marshall Cavendish Benchmark. He lives in New York City with his wife and daughter.